IMAGES
of America

BRIDGTON

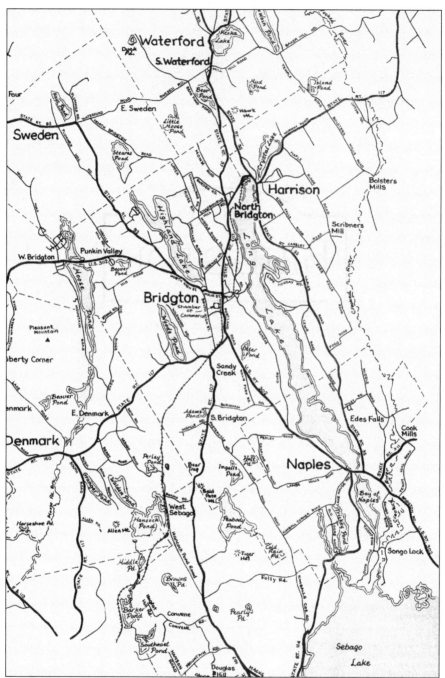

Map of Bridgton and Surrounding Area. This map was hand drawn and lettered by Martin P. Dombrowski.

On the cover: **Livery Stable on Bacon Street.** This photograph was probably taken during the first decade of the 20th century. This livery stable, which provided horses and carriages for hire, was located behind the Cumberland House hotel on Main Street. (Courtesy Bridgton Historical Society.)

IMAGES
of America

BRIDGTON

Ned Allen

ARCADIA
PUBLISHING

Published by Arcadia Publishing
Charleston, South Carolina

Library of Congress Catalog Card Number: 2008926689

For all general information contact Arcadia Publishing at:
Telephone 843-853-2070
Fax 843-853-0044
E-mail sales@arcadiapublishing.com
For customer service and orders:
Toll-Free 1-888-313-2665

Visit us on the Internet at www.arcadiapublishing.com

To all those members of the Bridgton Historical Society whose tireless work for over five decades has made this book possible.

CONTENTS

ACKNOWLEDGMENTS

Except where noted otherwise, the images in this book are from the Bridgton Historical Society collections, and without the work of the people who founded that organization and keep it going, this book would certainly not have been possible. I want to single out a few deserving individuals who have made exceptional contributions to that work. First and foremost, I must thank Eula Shorey, who edited the first Bridgton history, published in 1968. That work and its 1994 update provided the research base that has preserved so much of the town's history. Blynn Davis and Guy Monk, who are no longer with us, also made indispensable contributions to that body of knowledge.

Judith Blake, who left us far too early, did a masterful job pulling together our knowledge of Main Street, and Tom Johnson's work at the society in the 1980s, as well as Evelyn Lamb's ongoing contributions, have kept the society a vital organization. Thanks also to Margaret Reimer for graciously making her family's photograph collection available and, along with the rest of the board of trustees, ensuring that the society's business continued without a hitch while I was occupied with the writing of this book.

Hilary Zusman of Arcadia Publishing could not have been more supportive, helpful, and responsive when I had questions or problems. I also want to thank Nancy Smoak of the Rufus Porter Museum for the time she spent helping me during a very busy period. Finally, I must thank my wife, Carol Colby, for her support and understanding of the time I spent at the computer and the society trying to make sure this book does justice to its subject.

INTRODUCTION

Some people call Bridgton home, and others know it as the closest town to buy groceries and run errands. Many more probably know it as a town they pass through on the way to the Fryeburg Fair or the White Mountains. They drive up busy Main Street, which retains much of its historic, small-town character, and perhaps notice the town beach at the foot of Highland Lake. They may barely notice when they cross Stevens Brook, about 20 feet wide, and they are almost certainly unaware that in the latter part of the 19th century, Bridgton was full of busy mills that operated on the 10 power sites that the one-and-a-half-mile brook created.

In the 1760s, what is now Bridgton was in a wild, unsettled frontier area known as "Pondicherry." At that time, Maine was still part of Colonial Massachusetts. Although there had been Native American trails and settlements in the area, the Native Americans' presence does not seem to have figured much in the history of the white men's settlement of Bridgton. In 1765, the Massachusetts legislature approved a request by a group of men to develop a township here, adjacent to that of Col. Joseph Frye (Fryeburg). The land was granted in recognition of past military service. This group, known as the "proprietors," was led by Moody Bridges. In 1766, Solomon Wood led a surveying party to lay out the boundaries, and "Bridge's Town," eventually to be shortened to "Bridgton," was created.

Jacob Kimball, the first white settler, moved to the west shore of Long Pond (or Long Lake as it is now known), in North Bridgton, in 1768. Kimball, a former sea captain, operated a boat for passengers and freight from Standish, then known as Pearsontown, at the southern end of Sebago Lake. This was the most efficient way to reach Bridgton in those early years, when roads were little more than a track through the woods. A bit to the south of Kimball's settlement, Jacob Stevens settled on a little brook connecting Crotched Pond (now Highland Lake) and Long Lake. The proprietors had granted him land and water rights on the brook, on the condition that he establish a sawmill and gristmill. The brook that was named for him became one of the engines that drove the town's economy in the years to come.

But in those early years, most of the settlers were clearing forestland to create farms. Spreading out from North Bridgton, where Kimball had first settled, some early settlers developed farms on the land overlooking Crotched Pond, known most commonly as the "Ridge," or later in the 19th century, "Bridgton Highlands," a name more congenial to the summer visitors who began to populate the town. Other early settlers arrived in the southern portion of town. South Bridgton, approximately eight miles from the center village, was hilly, and many of the early farms were located on high ground. Although the soils in such areas were rather thin and became depleted in the 19th century, they had the advantage of being well-drained in the spring and less susceptible to frost than lower-lying areas.

Although Stevens's early mills on Stevens Brook were at the inlet where it flows into Long Lake, major development started at the other end of the brook, where it empties out of Highland Lake. The exact history of Bridgton's early industrial development is not entirely clear, but we know that a sawmill was built here at the foot of Highland Lake, known as the first power site, in 1788, and by the 1840s, a number of substantial mills were operating along the brook in the center village. By the latter part of the 19th century, there were 10 different power sites in use. Bridgton had become a busy, moderately-sized manufacturing center, with a tannery and corn-canning plant, factories turning out lumber, furniture, building materials, and other finished wood products, textiles, shoes, and machinery.

North Bridgton also had its share of manufacturing activity. In 1849, Luke Brown moved to Bridgton from Boston, where he had been a carpenter. He purchased the Beamon Mill in North Bridgton and established a furniture business. His sons Freeman and George eventually took over the company, which operated under the name Luke and F. H. Brown after 1878. It was known for making spool furniture, and it prospered for many years. In 1898, the company was sold to Horace Proctor of Harrison, who used it only as a sawmill. Nearby on the shores of Long Lake, Richard Kitson, and then his son Richard T. Kitson, produced pottery from the native clay for most of the 19th century. They made primarily utilitarian redware pieces, typically with a greenish interior glaze.

Bridgton also became a center for commercial activity in the region as retail stores, banks, and other businesses grew up to support the industrial workers in the village and farm families in outlying areas. In 1870, Maj. Henry A. Shorey founded the *Bridgton News*, which remains Bridgton's weekly newspaper and one of the area's key means of communication to this day. Remarkably it is still published by the Shorey family.

In January 1883, the first train on the narrow-gauge Bridgton and Saco River Railroad chugged into town, signaling the start of a new era. Until that time, the most efficient way to transport freight was still by boat, up through Sebago and Long Lakes. An important part of this link in the early days was the Walker log slip, built by Joseph Walker. It was apparently a series of ditches or sluices that enabled timber to be floated around the dams and falls on Stevens Brook, connecting to Long Lake. This enterprise formed the foundation for the Walker family's considerable industrial enterprises in 19th-century Bridgton. Water transport to the Lake Region was greatly improved with the opening of the Cumberland and Oxford Canal in 1830, which created a direct connection with Portland Harbor. It served the area well for several decades, but by the late 1850s, it was unable to compete with railroads.

The railroad connected to the standard-gauge Maine Central Railroad in Hiram. Since the narrow-gauge rails were just two feet apart, as opposed to standard gauge, which is over four and a half feet, to transfer freight, cars had to be off-loaded from one to the other on parallel sidings in Hiram. Even so, the line was an important link for the Bridgton-Lakes Region area, connecting it to the outside world for both freight and passengers. Narrow-gauge lines also had several advantages: they were cheaper to build and maintain and could wind around tighter turns. Until the internal combustion engine fully replaced animal power, the railroad provided a nearly essential means of transporting agricultural and forest products, as well as the textiles and other manufactured goods that were produced in Bridgton's mills.

In 1898, the line was extended from Bridgton to Harrison, at the northern end of Long Lake. The Maine Central Railroad purchased the line in 1912, but by the 1920s, competition from trucks and buses severely cut into the railroad's financial well-being. Reorganized in 1927 as the Bridgton and Harrison Railroad, it operated until 1941, when the equipment was sold and the track torn up and sold for scrap. Much of the rolling stock went to the Edaville Railroad, an outdoor museum in Massachusetts, and is now on display and in use at the Narrow Gauge Railroad Company and Museum in Portland.

The railroad also made the town more accessible to summer visitors, and tourism has played an important role since the late 19th century, when "rusticators" first started to appear during the summer months. Several substantial hotels were built in town, most notably the Bridgton

House and the Cumberland House hotel. There was even a hotel on top of Pleasant Mountain, accessible by either walking or riding up the carriage road. Other visitors stayed as boarders with farm families and at inns that sprang up near the lakes, and still others camped in tents. Some areas began as a camping area, but as time went on the tents were replaced by cabins. In Ingalls Grove on Highland Lake, for example, many of the same families returned year after year to lots they leased, built small cabins and cottages, and eventually obtained title to the land. Bridgton also became a popular spot for the establishment of children's summer camps, a tradition that continues, if to a somewhat lesser degree, today. In 1926, a golf course, designed by renowned golf course designer A. W. Tillinghast, was built on the Ridge, and the Bridgton Highlands Country Club is still going strong.

A number of visual and performing artists also discovered Bridgton around the beginning of the 20th century. An important although under-appreciated Maine artist, Charles Lewis Fox started spending summers on the Ridge, running an informal art school with his friend and fellow artist Curtis Perry. Metropolitan Opera star Olive Fremstad also had a summer home on Highland Lake in the second and third decades of the 20th century. Such well-known figures in the arts found themselves in a town that was appreciative of their work, with a tradition of community bands, musical groups, and amateur theater. Rufus Porter, who was born in 1792 and spent a portion of his childhood in the Bridgton area, decorated the walls of several local houses with the murals that he is so famous for. The newly founded Rufus Porter Museum preserves some of these murals in a house on North High Street that tells the story of this fascinating man's life and presents other aspects of his work and that of other folk artists.

Bridgton has valued education since its earliest days, when the first town meeting, held in 1794, approved plans for a school district and began raising money for buildings and teachers. In 1808, the town was starting to feel the need for a school that would provide education beyond that of the grammar schools, and a committee was formed to create such an institution. Three men, Samuel Andrews from North Bridgton, Enoch Perley from South Bridgton, and Dr. Samuel Farnsworth of the center village, contributed $500 apiece and raised a total of $5,000 to build an academy. Perhaps the hardest part of this process was choosing a site for the new school, and controversy erupted. It was finally decided that it would be built in North Bridgton, the factions came together to support the effort and the first classes were held in 1811. In 1872, Bridgton opened its public high school on Gibbs Avenue in the center village. Even then, many students continued to attend Bridgton Academy.

Today the academy continues to operate as a postsecondary school for boys, and in 1969, the high school was replaced by Lake Region High School, part of School Administrative District 61, which also includes the towns of Casco, Naples, and Sebago. Even the original high school building is now gone; despite efforts to find alternative uses, its condition had deteriorated to the point that the decision was made to tear it down in 1990.

Community theater was a very important part of life in Bridgton well into the 20th century. One group, the Highland Dramatics club, was founded around 1895 and continued to put on plays for another 50 years or so. These were typically performed at the opera house as fund-raisers for one or more local groups, and often the show went on the road to neighboring towns. In the 20th century, these amateur productions were supplemented in the summer by visits from groups of touring professionals.

Musical entertainment in Bridgton followed a similar pattern. During the 19th century, a number of musical clubs were formed, putting on concerts, recitals, and soirees of various sorts. In addition to Olive Fremstad's Bridgton summer home, the presence in nearby Harrison of Frederick Bristol, one of the leading musical teachers of his day, along with prominent pupils such as Marie Sundelius, brought professional musicians to the scene as well. The Saco Valley Music Festival, which featured Fremstad, Sundelius, and other nationally famous soloists, was an annual event for much of the second and third decades of the 20th century.

As the 20th century arrived and wore on, moving pictures became an important part of entertainment in and around Bridgton. The first silent movie in Bridgton was screened at the opera house, probably in 1913. A few years later, the Loyal Order of the Redmen bought the Grange hall on Depot Street and opened a second movie theater, the Riverside, on the ground floor (they used the second floor for their own meetings). By 1931, the Meserve Theater, later known as the Mayfair, the Brookside, and finally, the Magic Lantern, had opened on the site of the old tannery building in Post Office Square. Finally in 1935, Clarence "Dutch" Millet, the manager of the Mayfair, opened the State Theater at the corner of Main and Elm Streets. It operated until 1969, when the roof collapsed under the weight of a heavy snowstorm.

By the dawn of 21st century, it was determined that the old Magic Lantern building was sinking irretrievably into the unstable soil on which it was built, and Down East Industries, which owned it, determined that there was no alternative to tearing it down and building a replacement. In early 2008, the brand new theater, with three screens plus a pub area for live music, televised sports, and other special and community events, was opened. Along with the Bridgton Drive In, which opened in 1956, moviegoers in Bridgton have many choices available.

Bridgton's story is one of growth, change, and adaptation, but as the 21st century nears the end of its first decade, there is at least a cautious optimism about the town's future. Reny's Department Store has greatly expanded just across the street from the new Magic Lantern, and Hannaford Brothers opened a supermarket on Portland Street, right across from a large new Hancock Lumber store. Shawnee Peak, which is the oldest continuously operating ski area in Maine, has the largest night skiing operation in New England, which, along with snowmobiling, keeps things going in the winter.

Culturally, along with the new Rufus Porter Museum, Gallery 302 on Main Street shows the work of local artists, and the Bridgton Historical Society, which supplied nearly all of the images for this book, continues to strengthen its offerings at the museum in the old fire station and Narramissic, the Peabody-Fitch farm in South Bridgton.

This book is a visual portrait of the town, and by its nature, it cannot be, or claim to be, a comprehensive history. That task has already been accomplished, and it took 900 pages in a book published by the Bridgton Historical Society. No doubt there are people and events that get less attention than they deserve, but it is hoped that readers will get an entertaining and informative glimpse of what made Bridgton what it was in the past and what it is today.

One

ROADS, RAILS, AND WATERWAYS
THE STORY OF TRANSPORTATION IN BRIDGTON

WEST COVE, C. 1830. This painting by John Mead II depicts the site where Capt. Benjamin Kimball established Bridgton's first settlement. It is now Bridgton Academy's beach. Kimball was granted land on the condition that he establish a store and tavern and provide a sailboat to transport passengers and freight from Pearsontown (now Standish) at the southern end of Sebago Lake. In those early days, roads were nearly nonexistent.

PLUMMER'S LANDING, C. 1870. This is an early photograph of Plummer's Landing on Long Lake, one of the main points of entry into Bridgton when boats were a major mode of transportation. The vessel on the right appears to be one of the boats that plied the waters of the Cumberland and Oxford Canal. These two-masted boats were 65 feet long and 10 feet wide with square bottoms. The canal itself, which opened in 1830, was approximately 20 miles long but connected through Sebago Lake, Brandy Pond, and Long Lake all the way to Harrison, about 50 miles inland. At its peak, as many as 150 boats traveled the canal. Typically the boats were manned by a captain and two crew members and carried 25–30 tons of freight, although they were known to carry as much as 60 tons. The canal prospered for several decades, but by the late 1850s, competition from railroads forced it into bankruptcy. Canal Bank, which had been formed to finance its construction, took over and sold it to new operators, who kept it open until 1870.

STEAMER HAWTHORNE ON LONG LAKE. The Sebago and Long Lake Steamship Company operated steamers to transport freight on the lakes starting around 1840. When the lakes were frozen they carried the freight on stagecoaches. In 1846, the Sebago and Long Pond Steam Navigation Company was formed, and in 1847, it launched the *Fawn*, a side-wheeler that was the first passenger steamship on the lakes. She was built in North Bridgton for a cost of $8,000 and carried passengers to meet the stage to Portland at Standish. Other early side-wheelers were the *Oriental*, the *Sebago*, and the *Mount Pleasant*. In 1873, when the *Sebago* burned at the landing in Bridgton, she was replaced with the screw-propelled *Hawthorne*, shown here, which operated for 35 years. Other steamships that operated on the lakes were the *Goodridge*, *Worrambus*, *Songo*, *Sokokis*, *Hiawatha*, *Minnehaha*, and the *Bay of Naples*. Regular service on a daily schedule was discontinued in 1932.

EXCURSION

-- TO --

PORTLAND

Over Sebago Lake Route.

TUESDAY & WEDNESDAY,

JUNE 22d & 23d.

Tickets will be sold over Sebago Lake Route to Portland and return Tuesday and Wednesday 22d and 23d, good to **return on Thursday, June 24th.**

WEDNESDAY, JUNE 23,

STEAMER SEBAGO will leave Harrison at **3.45**, North Bridgton **4.00**, Bridgton **4.30**, and Naples **5.15 A. M.**, returning on regular time.

June 22d and 24th Steamer will run on regular advertised time.

TICKETS FOR ROUND TRIP, $1.50.

SEBAGO STEAMBOAT CO.

Bridgton, June 18, '80.

PORTLAND EXCURSION BROADSIDE. Although land transportation to Bridgton was greatly improved by 1880, steamships continued to play a role. They were particularly popular with summer visitors, who used them both as transportation to get to their vacation destination and as a pleasurable excursion. Often the boats would be met by the train in Standish, which connected to Portland, and from there to Boston. It was actually possible to take a train from Boston to Sebago Lake Station in Standish, a steamer up the lakes to Bridgton, then the narrow-gauge railroad to Bridgton Junction in Hiram, where passengers could board a train and return to Boston via Portland. The excursion advertised in this broadside from the Bridgton Historical Society archives is the type of excursion that the poet Henry Wadsworth Longfellow took in 1875 when he visited Bridgton. The historical society also has the hotel register from the Bridgton House that Longfellow signed. His poem *The Songo River*, which describes the narrow twisting river that connects Sebago Lake with Long Lake, was apparently written about this trip.

14

BAY OF NAPLES AND GOODRIDGE. The *Bay of Naples*, seen here approaching North Bridgton around 1900, was built in 1906 in Racine, Wisconsin. She was then disassembled and shipped to Naples, Maine, and reassembled. She gave good service until 1931, when she burned. The next year the steamer *Goodridge*, seen below also approaching North Bridgton, also burned. The two charred hulks remained in view for several years, until a Depression-era public works project removed them. The *Songo River Queen* continues to provide tourist excursions on the lakes, but her future is uncertain at the time of this writing. The swing bridge on the Naples causeway needs to be replaced, and budgetary constraints may mean that it will be replaced with a fixed bridge. A vessel the size of the *Songo River Queen* could not pass under such a bridge.

Steamboat Landing, Bridgton, Me.

4288-PUBLISHED BY G. A. CABOT. "THE BRIDGTON"

STAGECOACH AT STEAMBOAT LANDING. By 1815, there was a regularly scheduled stage line from Norway to Portland, passing through Bridgton. It was a slow and uncomfortable means of transportation; one early traveler reported that it took more than three days to go from Bridgton to Portland in an 1837 winter storm. Nevertheless the stage continued to be an important link in the transportation system even into the 20th century. Travelers could arrive by train or, as in these pictures, boat and be met by a stagecoach to get into town or their hotel. Both of these photographs were probably taken around 1905. In the image below, the smokestack of the steamer and what appears to be part of her superstructure is visible on the far left. From this, it appears to be the *Songo*, which was built in 1904.

Marshall Bacon and the Cumberland House Livery Stable. This is a photograph of Marshall Bacon, owner of the Cumberland House's livery stable, proudly showing off two of the stable's horses. A 1914 Sanborn Insurance Company map shows a building on this site (possibly the same one) as being part of the hotel but not a stable. The same map shows a livery stable just across the bridge on the other side of Bacon Street, and it is this latter building that is shown on the cover of this book. Livery stables, which boarded horses and provided horses and carriages for hire, performed an important service in the days before automobiles. There were several in Bridgton. Not surprisingly, one was located near the railroad station, which would be somewhat analogous to car rental agencies found today near airports. By this time, Bridgton was already a popular destination for many summer visitors. They would arrive by train and have a source of transportation to take them to their final destination.

SHOWING OFF THE FAMILY HORSE AND CARRIAGE. Eunice Smith Haynes poses with a very smart-looking four-wheel carriage and horse for the picture above. Haynes was the daughter of Benjamin Franklin Smith, who lived on the Middle Ridge Road in Bridgton. The photograph below was taken on the Hio Ridge Road in the western part of Bridgton, with the shoulder of Pleasant Mountain in the background. The individuals are unidentified. An impressive horse and carriage must have been a source of great pride, judging from the large number of similar images in the Bridgton Historical Society archives, with subjects usually posed in their Sunday best.

PONDICHERRY SQUARE IN THE EARLY 20TH CENTURY. The back of this postcard from the early 1900s is labeled "Saturday shopping—Pondicherry Square." The buildings on the left may still stand much as they appear here, but the traffic on Main Street, which is also busy Route 302, is very different. The automobile in the background illustrates the transition that was taking place in land transportation during that era.

PERLEY FROST AND IKE. Although many people today love their automobiles, and occasionally even name them, it is hard to imagine having quite the same relationship with a car as with a horse. Here Perley Frost gives his 26-year-old horse, Ike, a glass of ginger ale, while Walter Hawkins looks on. Frost had been giving Ike soda pop since he was a colt. (Photograph by Arthur Griffin, courtesy Bridgton Historical Society.)

A "GALAMANDER." This rugged horse-drawn work vehicle was designed to haul logs from Highland Lake to the sawmill, probably the Bisbee sawmill off lower Main Street. Here it is being driven down Main Street hill (the tower of the Gibbs Mill is visible on the far left) by Elisha Heath.

HORSE-DRAWN WORK SLEIGH. This photograph was taken at the James Chadbourne farm in North Bridgton. Many farmers turned to logging or some form of home industry to make ends meet in the winter months. In the days before motorized vehicles, it was often easier to haul heavy loads on vehicles with runners in winter than on wheeled vehicles at other times of year.

OUTSIDE THE OLD POST OFFICE. This photograph was taken outside the post office when it was at the corner of Main and Nulty Streets. This building replaced the original Staples Block, which burned in 1898. The post office remained here until 1921, when it moved across the street to the Knights of Pythias Block.

THE FAMILY SLEIGH. Of course, horse-drawn sleighs were not used only as work vehicles. Here a family poses outside their home, bundled against the winter cold. This open sleigh without sides appears to leave the occupants rather exposed to the elements and seems out of character with the elaborate, fashionable hats the ladies are wearing.

ENGINE AT BRIDGTON YARD. The Bridgton and Saco River Railroad (later renamed the Bridgton and Harrison), a narrow-gauge line, was chartered in 1882. There were several competing ideas regarding what route it was to follow, but after much debate, it was decided that it should connect to the standard-gauge Maine Central Railroad in Hiram, a distance of about 15 miles. On January 31, 1883, the first train came into town, with two round trips daily, taking about an hour and 15 minutes each way. The line was an important link for the Bridgton-Lakes Region area, connecting it to the outside world for both freight and passengers. Without it, it would have been very difficult for the busy Bridgton mills to import any raw materials not locally available or to ship their finished products to market. The line operated eight different engines during the nearly 60 years of service. These little engines belching black smoke and steam were a familiar sight during that period, symbolizing a degree of prosperity for the town and surrounding areas.

INTERIOR OF NARROW-GAUGE RAILWAY CAR. The railroad also made the area more accessible for vacationers, and for several decades, this would have been the way most visitors arrived in Bridgton. This view of the interior of a passenger car illustrates the small size of the narrow gauge, which operated on rails just two feet apart, as opposed to the four feet, eight and a half inches that separate standard rails.

RAILROAD TICKETS, 1899. These tickets were all stamped on the back with dates from the summer of 1899. The Maine Central Railroad provided passage from Portland to Bridgton Junction in Hiram, where passengers and freight transferred to the tiny narrow gauge to complete the trip to Bridgton. The smaller narrow gauge was more economical to construct and operate and could maneuver around tighter curves than the larger standard gauge.

NORTH BRIDGTON RAILROAD STATION, AUGUST 1904. The railroad prospered for several decades, and in 1898, it was extended from Bridgton to Harrison, a distance of a little over five miles, with a station in North Bridgton, shown here. This was undertaken at least in part in response to proposals to extend trolley service from Portland through Westbrook, all the way up the east shore of Sebago Lake and on to Harrison, and a similar proposal to link the Norway and Paris Street Railway to Waterford. Neither of these plans ever came to fruition. In 1921, its peak year, the narrow-gauge railroad line reported earning $113,000; within a very few years, however, this situation was reversed, and in 1930 financial difficulties forced the closure of both the North Bridgton and Harrison stations. Ironically this was also when the Bridgton and Saco River Railroad was taken over by a new owner and became known as the Bridgton and Harrison Railroad.

STOPPING FOR MAIL AT SANDY CREEK. The Bridgton and Saco River Railroad was an important link for the small towns and hamlets along its route. There were seven different stations between Bridgton and Hiram. Here the train is in Sandy Creek, the last stop before Bridgton, delivering mail. At one time, there were small post offices in nearly all of these outlying neighborhoods.

BRIDGTON RAIL YARD, 1940. This is a view of the railroad yard in Bridgton, looking back toward town and the passenger terminal. This photograph was taken in the last days of the line's existence, a year before it was permanently shut down. The grandstand on the right, built in 1934 with money from the Works Progress Administration (WPA), served the school's athletic field for many years.

RAILROAD TERMINAL, C. 1941. For many years, the railroad terminal, located on Depot Street near the site of the present elementary school, was one of Bridgton's most important links with the rest of the world. However, by the 1920s, the rise of the automobile brought mounting financial troubles for the railroad, and by the time this photograph was taken, its days were numbered. (Courtesy Allen P. Richmond III.)

RAILBUS AT BRIDGTON STATION. As an economy move, in 1930, the railroad began running a hybrid vehicle, known as a railbus. This ungainly vehicle was improvised from a 1927 Chevrolet sedan. In 1936, the line acquired a far superior railbus from the Sandy River Railroad. The three-axle machine, with its boxcar trailer, proved to be an economical way to operate the line in its last years.

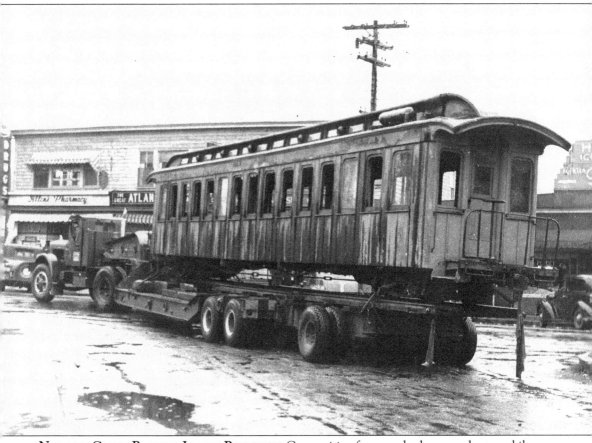

NARROW-GAUGE RAILWAY LEAVES BRIDGTON. Competition from trucks, buses, and automobiles placed a heavy burden on the little railroad. Despite the more efficient railbus and the determined efforts of the line to stay in business, by 1941, the Bridgton and Harrison Railroad had reached the end of the line and was put up for auction. The track was pulled up almost immediately and sold for scrap. Much of the equipment and rolling stock was sold to Ellis Atwood, who operated the Edaville Railroad, a narrow-gauge tourist attraction in Carver, Massachusetts, for many years. However, in 1993, that business sold much of its equipment, including the Bridgton and Saco River engines, Nos. 7 and 8, to the Maine Narrow Gauge Railroad Company and Museum in Portland. Located at the site of the Portland Company on Fore Street, this organization preserves Maine's industrial and railroading heritage, running trains around the Portland waterfront on a regular basis. At the time of this writing, there are serious discussions about bringing some of that equipment back to Bridgton as well.

SEARS AUTOMOBILE, 1911. This car, the first in the Hio neighborhood, was purchased by the Cook family for about $500. It arrived at the railroad station in crates with some assembly required. The Cooks frequently drove it in parades and celebrations, as pictured here, and apparently it even climbed Mount Washington. In 1985, the family donated it to the Bridgton Historical Society, where it remains on permanent display.

MOOSE POND CAUSEWAY, 1920s. It is unclear how early settlers traversed Moose Pond to travel between Bridgton and Fryeburg, although the first bridge across the end of the pond was built in the 1830s. With advances in transportation, particularly the advent of the automobile, a more substantial structure with a hard-surface was needed. Major projects to upgrade the structure, part of Route 302, were undertaken in 1923 and 1953.

MOOSE POND CAUSEWAY CONSTRUCTION, 1923. The first step was to add rock and gravel fill to the existing bridge structure, which was originally much closer to the water level. This created a wider base, resulting in a causeway 24 feet wide, with 18 feet of blacktop and a 3-foot shoulder. The 1951 construction went a step further, creating a 24-foot-wide road with 8-foot shoulders on each side.

MOOSE POND BRIDGE UNDER CONSTRUCTION. The only part of the causeway that can truly be termed a bridge was originally a sluiceway for logs. Here an iron bridge built in 1900 is being replaced. The upper structure was actually a temporary bridge that allowed traffic to pass during construction. One bus driver refused to cross it and detoured through Sweden and Lovell, a distance of approximately 14 miles.

CONSTRUCTION MISHAP, MOOSE POND CAUSEWAY, 1923. Obviously the causeway construction in 1923 was not without its problems. Although the details have been lost, these photographs tell a fairly clear and compelling story. The dump truck, apparently providing some of the rock fill for the construction, apparently got too close to the edge and tumbled into Moose Pond. Unfortunately it is not known if this was anything worse than an embarrassing incident for the driver, but one hopes that it was brought to a happy end by this steam shovel.

SERVICE STATIONS. As gasoline engines replaced horses, gasoline service stations began to appear in Bridgton. Today few repair shops sell gasoline, and most gasoline is sold at convenience stores. But like most service stations in 1924, when the photograph above was taken, the Bridgton Garage on Portland Street (better known today as Route 302) did both, selling gasoline and performing automobile repairs. The back of this photograph identifies the men as, from left to right, "Yours Truly, Warren Benton, Father Foster, Bill Foster, and Biggy Smith." The American Oil Company (Amoco) Station at the right was also on Portland Street. The back of the photograph identifies the man as Bill Harmon, taken around 1939. The Amoco courtesy cards advertised in the sign are examples of some of the first credit cards, which were issued by companies selling gasoline.

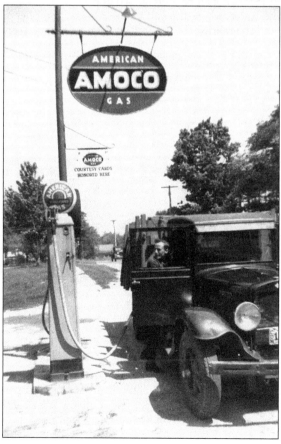

BIPLANE IN FRONT OF BRIDGTON HOUSE, C. 1913. Bridgton has never had an airport, although in 1871, a hot air balloon landed in front of the Bridgton House and barnstormers used to fly into the Ridge, where the golf course now is, and offer rides. The traveling exhibit of this biplane (and the touring car that towed it) caused quite a sensation when it stopped in town.

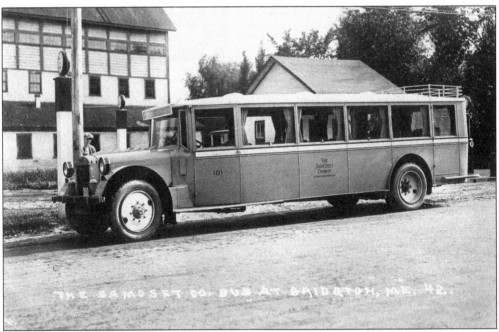

SAMOSET BUS, C. 1927. The Samoset Bus Company operated service between Portland and Bridgton from 1925 to 1930. The company was a subsidiary of the Maine Central Railroad. Here the vehicle is parked on Main Street, in front of the old tannery building just a few years before it was torn down.

32

Two

MAKING A LIVING
BUSINESS, COMMERCE,
AND AGRICULTURE

FOOT OF HIGHLAND LAKE, C. 1875. This is the outlet of Highland Lake (originally known as Crotched Pond), the start of Stevens Brook. Although in 1768, the proprietors granted Jacob Stevens "the privilege of building a dam at the outlet of Crotched Pond," he actually built the first mill at the other end, where the brook empties into Long Lake. Nevertheless the village center developed from the Highland Lake end.

OUTLET OF HIGHLAND LAKE. This photograph was taken looking back across the outlet of Stevens Brook, the backbone of Bridgton's industrial development, toward Main Hill from an area near the present town beach. The foreground is the area that is now Shorey Park, but the dam here provided power for several different mills. By the 1790s, there was a sawmill operating here, with a gristmill nearby, both owned by William Sears. Sears had moved to Bridgton from Beverly, Massachusetts, in 1789 and purchased the property and water rights from Asa Kimball over a period of several years. By the time this photograph was taken, the power site was occupied by Gibbs Mill, which, with its distinctive tower, is visible on the left. The building on the far right is the Gibbs Opera House, which stood in "the fork" on Main Street, which was eliminated when Shorey Park was created.

GIBBS MILL. Rufus Gibbs (1800–1892), one of Bridgton's leading businessmen, got his start at Maj. Thomas Perley's tannery in South Bridgton and later established his own tannery. He owned a great deal of property and controlled the first two power sites on Stevens Brook, operating a woolen mill, sawmill, and a shingle mill. He was one of the founders of the first bank in Bridgton and served in the Maine legislature in 1879. This mill was built by Rufus Gibbs and John Hall in 1857. Gibbs bought out Hall's interest in 1858. The mill, which was known variously as the Cumberland Mill and the Little Gibbs Mill, was capable of turning out 200–250 wool blankets a day and did a very brisk business with the United States government during the Civil War. It was torn down in 1941.

THE PONDICHERRY WOOLEN MILL. This large building is shown here in the early 20th century, probably around 1920, at a time when it was already past its prime as a productive manufacturing facility. It was built in 1865 by Frederick J. Littlefield and his two brothers-in-law Alvin Davis and Frederick Storer. In 1873, Rufus Gibbs, who was related to Littlefield, organized the Pondicherry Company (as opposed to the Pondicherry Mills Company) and took over this mill. The new company operated both the Pondicherry Mill and the smaller Little Gibbs Mill on Main Hill. According to the 1904 *Bridgton Town Register*, between the two mills, the company had 60 looms in operation and produced 18,000 yards of cloth per week. The Pondicherry Company had 225 employees and a $7,000 monthly payroll. Clearly it made an important contribution to Bridgton's economy.

PONDICHERRY MILL INTERIOR. This photograph illustrates the impressive industrial machinery at the heart of Bridgton's woolen industry. Hundreds of bobbins of yarn were spun by machinery powered by belts on pulleys overhead. By the late 1890s, the machinery demanded more power than Stevens Brook could provide. The 100-foot tower was built, and the switch was made to coal. The building was torn down in 1965. Food City now occupies the site.

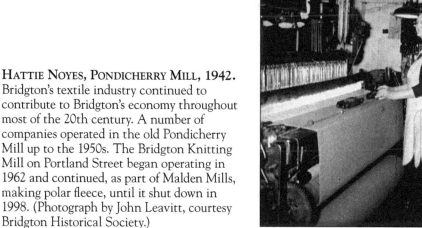

HATTIE NOYES, PONDICHERRY MILL, 1942. Bridgton's textile industry continued to contribute to Bridgton's economy throughout most of the 20th century. A number of companies operated in the old Pondicherry Mill up to the 1950s. The Bridgton Knitting Mill on Portland Street began operating in 1962 and continued, as part of Malden Mills, making polar fleece, until it shut down in 1998. (Photograph by John Leavitt, courtesy Bridgton Historical Society.)

CORN PACKING PLANT. In 1865, the J. Winslow Jones Corn Packing Company built a corn-packing plant on the corner of Main and Elm Streets. It was a large, sprawling complex, extending back as far as the present post office. Albion Hall Burnham, originally from Harrison, worked for J. Winslow Jones in his Portland-area plants for many years, acquiring a thorough knowledge of the business. When Jones decided to open a plant in Bridgton, he made Burnham its general manager. The land was extremely wet, described by some as a swamp, but the factory

remained there until 1889, when it moved to Depot Street, on the current site of the Bridgton Community Center. One advantage to this new site was that it was very close to the railroad station. Burnham, who eventually came to own the firm when it became the Bridgton Canning Company, was a very successful businessman. After his death in 1902, the company was sold to the Burnham and Morrill Company. At that time, it employed approximately 100 workers and was said to do an annual business of $350,000.

THE TANNERY. The tanning of animal hides into leather was a useful process for the early settlers, and the tanning industry was an important one in Bridgton for much of the 19th century. It was a logical adjunct to Bridgton's agricultural business, providing another market for the forest products and animal products farmers produced. In Bridgton, the tannin used was derived mostly from hemlock bark, which was present in abundance at the time. Often the farmers would pay by some version of the barter system. For example, in 1836, Augustus Perley tanned three calfskins for Joseph Ingalls and took one for his pay. There were a number of different tanneries in Bridgton at various times, but this was the largest. The first tannery at this site (by Tannery Bridge, now the site of the Magic Lantern) was built by Rufus Gibbs in 1836. It burned in 1855, and its replacement burned in 1893. This structure replaced it. At its height, this tannery employed as many as 50 men, using 10,000 cords of bark to process 8,000–10,000 hides per year.

FOREST MILLS. In 1861, William Perry and George Taylor purchased a large tract of land on both sides of Stevens Brook in the lower village, including the water rights at five different power sites. After Taylor died in 1878, the Forest Mills Company was organized to manage the company, and it was incorporated in 1879. Although it was a sprawling complex on the lower section of Stevens Brook, some details of the company's history remain sketchy. It is amazing how little evidence of this massive enterprise, located on Mill Street, remains. Today even the crumbling remains shown here, photographed in 1965, are gone. While some of the stonework and parts of the dams can be seen, the area is now largely wooded. (Below, photograph by David M. Witham, courtesy Bridgton Historical Society.)

FOREST MILLS WORKERS. An early inscription on the back dates this photograph of textile workers to July 4, 1897. William Perry and George Taylor, who founded the Forest Mills Company, were primarily concerned with textile manufacturing, which they carried on at two of the power sites. They leased the water rights to the other power sites to other owners, who operated a machine shop, a foundry, and various woodworking mills.

WORKERS OUTSIDE THE STOCKING MILL, C. 1908. In 1865, Perry and Taylor purchased a stocking mill, which had been started in 1860. The workers posing here are, from left to right, (first row) Walter Keen, Enoch Sanborn, John Strout, unidentified, Perley Frost, Harry Driscoll, Fred Martin, and three unidentified; (second row) John Long, Del Martin, unidentified, Wrenn Kelley, Eddie Green, Joseph Leavitt, Tom Martin, Charles Weymouth, and William Lopeman Sr.

MILL HOUSING, LOWER MAIN STREET. Housing must have been in great demand for the hundreds of workers employed in the huge Forest Mills complex and the Pondicherry Woolen Mill in the lower village. In this photograph from around 1900, one of the families living in this two-family house on lower Main Street is posing outside in their yard. The Forest Mills Company owned two tenements nearby to house some of their many employees, who numbered 130 in 1903. No doubt this industrial activity spurred the residential development in this part of town. Mill Street was authorized by the town in 1864, extending to the Taylor and Perry boardinghouse at the corner of Oak Street, and in 1865, the town meeting appropriated money to build Kansas Road across Stevens Brook, at the site of the current bridge. The first construction of wooden sidewalks, on upper Main Street and High Street, was underwritten by prominent citizens in 1878. The sidewalks in this part of town were probably built somewhat later.

DAM ABOVE POWER STATION. The Bridgton Water and Electric Company was formed in the late 1890s. In February 1898, electricity became available in Bridgton, thanks to this dam, near the mouth of Stevens Brook, where it empties into Long Lake. Ironically, or perhaps fittingly, it is also near the site of the first dam in Bridgton, built by Jacob Stevens in 1768 to power his sawmill.

PENSTOCK CARRYING WATER TO POWER HOUSE. The large pipe here, known as a penstock, carried water from the dam to the powerhouse, where electricity was generated. These folks, all members of the Stubbs and Jury families, are apparently enjoying a recreational outing, anticipating the future use of this area, in the general vicinity of Salmon Point, where the town owns a campground, picnic area, and boat launch.

BRIDGTON MACHINE COMPANY AND THE PERRY TURBINE. In 1871, William Perry and George Taylor built three buildings for an iron foundry and machine shop to be operated by Samuel Miller and Richard T. Bailey, just above Forest Mills and across from the Smith Mill. In 1887, the company that Miller and Bailey founded became the Bridgton Machine Company, owned by Forest Mills and managed by George N. and Frank H. Burnham. The company produced water wheels, shingle machines, shafts, pulleys, and hangers. Its most important achievement was the Perry Turbine Water Wheel, apparently invented by the company's owner, William Fessenden Perry. It was a greatly improved, simple, rugged design for a turbine that greatly increased the efficiency of water-powered machinery, an appropriate product to be invented along the banks of Stevens Brook, which seemed to power so much industry with so little water.

THE PERRY

TURBINE.

DESCRIPTIVE CATALOGUE.

BRIDGTON MACHINE CO.,

BRIDGTON, - - - MAINE.

ESTABLISHED IN 1871.

SAWMILL ON LOWER STEVENS BROOK. This was another mill that, like the Bridgton Machine Company, was managed for the Forest Mills Company by George N. and Frank H. Burnham. Not surprisingly, the Burnhams were related to William Perry, one of the principals in Forest Mills. But when this photograph was taken, this mill, located off Mill Street just above the Smith Mill and the machine shop, was probably being operated by A. H. Harriman and Company. A. H. Harriman had leased it from the Forest Mills Company in 1884. It was not until 1899 that the Bridgton Lumber Company took over. By 1905, it employed 15 workers at two mills, one for long stock and one for short, and annually produced approximately a million board feet of lumber, along with boxes, finished architectural products, and other goods.

BISBEE SAWMILL FIRE. On July 27, 1953, the electric motor that powered the sawmill overheated and the building went up in flames. It burned so fiercely that it threatened the box factory on the other side of Stevens Brook. The owner, Harry Bisbee, in his late 80s, set up diesel-powered machinery nearby, but the company never really rebounded from the loss. (Photograph by Wilkins, Bridgton, courtesy Bridgton Historical Society.)

HARRY BISBEE. In 1920, Bisbee, originally from Sumner, Maine, bought the former Bridgton Lumber Company sawmill from the widows of Frank Burnham and Sumner Newcomb, who had purchased it in 1911. He operated the mill for decades, converting it to electricity from water power. Bisbee retired at the age of 92 in 1957 and passed away two years later, leaving a very generous bequest to the Bridgton Public Library.

SMITH MILL AND SHOWROOM. Before moving to Bridgton in 1868, Lewis Smith had a successful career in the furniture business, including a period with the well-known furniture maker Walter Corey in Portland. In Bridgton, Smith manufactured furniture, sash, blinds, doors, and other finished building components. Most important, he pioneered in the coffin-manufacturing business, and this mill above, the only old Bridgton mill building to survive into the 21st century, is often known as the "Coffin Shop." Smith built a large building at the lower corner of Depot and Main Streets in Pondicherry Square (below). The building burned on Easter morning (April 6) 1958. (Below, photograph by Allan C. Dodge, courtesy Bridgton Historical Society.)

KITSON POTTERY. From about 1815 to 1887, Richard Kitson and his son, Richard T. Kitson (right), operated a pottery on the shore of North Bridgton in the building on the left, above. Richard purchased the land, with the right to dig clay from the banks of the brook, in 1809. The clay proved suitable for making bricks and pottery, and for over 70 years, he and his son, who took over in 1859, turned out many redware items, usually with a distinctive greenish glaze on the inside. Most of the products were bowls, covered pots, milk pans, and other utilitarian household forms. According to U.S. census figures in 1850, they were using 20 cords of wood, 20 tons of clay, and 1,000 pounds of lead annually. (Right, courtesy Allen P. Richmond III.)

The National and Savings Bank, Bridgton Maine.

BANK BUILDING. This building's appearance has barely changed since it was built in 1907 to house the Bridgton Savings Bank, the Bridgton National Bank, and several others. From 1965 to 1989, it housed the town offices, with a courtroom and jail. In 2002, Oberg Insurance and Real Estate, which had occupied offices in the building at its founding in 1933, moved in.

OFFICER FOWLER, MAINE STATE POLICE. In the 1920s and 1930s, three Fowler brothers from Bridgton were members of the state highway police. This is most likely Bert Fowler, who was assigned to the Bridgton area. The town established its own police department in 1965, with Roger Pendexter as chief and two night officers. A police cruiser was also purchased.

FULLER BRUSH MAN. The identity of this salesman is not known, but the "Fuller Brush Man" was a familiar figure for decades in the 20th century. The company, which is still in business selling brushes and cleaning aids, was founded in 1906 by Alfred C. Fuller, who was originally from Canada. Traveling salesmen went door-to-door selling various types of brushes. Note the sign in the window for "ice," signaling that the household needed a delivery of ice for their ice chest. Electric refrigerators became available by the 1920s, but some households continued to use ice chests. In Bridgton, as elsewhere in New England, there was a long tradition of cutting ice on local lakes and ponds and storing it in sawdust for use all year. Kramer's Ice House, at the foot of Highland Lake, supplied ice until the mid-1940s, when the icehouse was torn down.

PONDICHERRY SQUARE. Another section of Main Street that remains readily recognizable in the old photographs is Pondicherry Square, where Route 302 takes a sharp turn up Main Street at the traffic light. Most of the commercial buildings on the left-hand side remain standing today. The building on the right is Lewis Smith's furniture and coffin showroom. This photograph was probably taken in the early 1880s, before Joseph Wales and John Hamblen acquired the building that is still known as Wales and Hamblen. Frank Gibbs sold crockery, dry goods, and paper hangings on the corner, and F. H. Bennett's apothecary can be seen on Portland Street facing the camera. The Wales and Hamblen building was already a hardware store, but not yet known by that name. Many of the businesses that occupied the building after the demise of the Wales and Hamblen hardware store continued to incorporate the Wales and Hamblen name in some form. The building is listed on the National Register of Historic Places.

JOSEPH WALES (RIGHT) AND JOHN HAMBLEN (BELOW). In 1891, these two men became partners in a hardware business, and their building on Main Street has been known as the Wales and Hamblen building ever since. They were, however, not the first to operate a hardware store in that location. Several buildings housed hardware stores there (the current one was built in 1882), with a succession of owners; Gibbs, Fowler and Wales became Fowler, Wales, and Goodwin. Following a fire, it was briefly known as Chandler and Wales, and then, in 1891, John Hamblen, a clerk in the store, bought an interest, and it became Wales and Hamblen.

CARRIAGE SHOP. The *Bridgton News* occupied this building in 1879, but this photograph may be earlier than that. The first floor was a blacksmith shop, which explains the wide doorway, where Thomas Dresser, Lewis and Jonathan Seavey, and John Webb practiced their trade. The second floor was Ansel Pratt's carriage-making shop. The man at the top of the ramp standing in front of the carriage wheel may be Pratt.

CENTRAL GARAGE, 1930S. Located between Bacon Street and Tannery Bridge, this was the 20th-century version of the carriage and blacksmith shop. It had been a garage and automobile showroom since 1914, having operated as a Ford dealership, which Ripley and Fletcher of South Paris bought in 1919. Later it was the town garage, information bureau, and state motor vehicle division. It was torn down for a parking lot in 1977.

MESERVE'S GARAGE. Many different businesses occupied this building through the years. In addition to the garage and theater, Dr. Fred Noble had his dental offices here; the Bridgton Dress Company, operated by Lee Cloutier; Western Auto, owned by Allan Hayes and Donald Cobb; William Severance's real estate office; Waterford Industries; M&M Alloy Castings; Howell Laboratories; the Bridgton Book House; and Downeast Industries have all occupied parts of the building.

MESERVE'S GARAGE INTERIOR. This was taken inside Claude Meserve's garage; Meserve is on the far right here. The young man on the left is Meserve's son Glenn; next to him are Kenneth Cobb and Carl Kilborn. The other man, next to Claude, is his son-in-law Carl Irish.

55

MESERVE'S GARAGE UNDER CONSTRUCTION, 1929. In 1929, the old tannery building at the corner of Depot Street and Main Street was in such a state of disrepair that it was beyond salvation. Claude Meserve purchased the property and built an automobile repair shop and showroom, with a theater on the second floor.

POST OFFICE SQUARE IN THE 1950S. This is opposite Reny's Department Store. Allen's Pharmacy is now Bridgton Books. Swansons' opened in 1940 and operated for many years under the ownership of John Swanson, then George Giatis, who bought the business in 1967. While the businesses have changed, and another new building now occupies the area between the Philco sign and the State Theater, this area is easily recognizable today.

GALLINARI FRUIT COMPANY ADVERTISING FAN. In 1907, Tony Gallinari left Italy for the United States. He accidentally ended up in Bridgton thanks to miscommunication with a railroad ticket agent, but he liked the town and stayed, opening a fruit stand. It grew into a successful business, and he purchased the store on Main Street next to Allen's Pharmacy. His family has been an important part of Bridgton ever since.

METHODIST HILL. The building on the right was Abbott's Dry Goods store, which burned in 1894. The second house down from the Methodist church, at the corner of Main and Chase Streets, is now the headquarters of the Lakes Environmental Association (LEA). Since its founding in 1970, the LEA has grown into a strong and highly respected organization working effectively to protect the quality of the region's lakes and waterways.

BENNETT'S PHARMACY. This building was constructed in 1898, replacing an earlier structure that housed a blacksmith shop and carriage shop. The Knights of Pythias hall was on the third floor, Bennett's Pharmacy and Hales Boot and Shoe Store occupied the ground level, and various offices were on the second floor. The building was rebuilt after a major fire that started across the street in 1906, and a ladies' apparel and gift shop occupied the building for many years. The first telephone switchboard was here in 1899, staffed by an operator who sat on a raised platform in the middle of the store. Since the operator was on hand to connect the 14 subscribers only when the store was open, telephone service depended on the store's schedule. In 1921, the post office moved in, occupying the space previously used by Bennett's Pharmacy. It stayed there until 1962, when the current post office was built.

RENY'S DEPARTMENT STORE.
Reny's Department Store, a small chain with stores in moderately sized towns throughout Maine, moved into the Knights of Pythias Block in 1952, just a year before the photograph on the right was taken. It has been a major presence on Main Street, and the Lakes Region, since then. In 2008, Reny's Department Store took over the adjacent property and built a huge addition. Coupled with the simultaneous rebuilding of the Magic Lantern Theater across Depot Street, this constituted the greatest transformation of the Post Office Square area in over a century. Even so, although little of the original fabrics survive, the general outlines of the old Knights of Pythias building on the corner can still be discerned under the vinyl siding.

SOUTH BRIDGTON BUSINESSES. Although agriculture in New England was becoming an increasingly difficult proposition in the late 19th and early 20th centuries, there were still many farms in outlying areas such as South Bridgton. But in those days, a trip into town was still more of an undertaking than it is today, and there were also small stores and businesses. Knapp and Sanborn (above) was one of two businesses (the Foster Brothers being the other one) listed in the 1896–1897 *Maine Register* that sold dry goods and groceries in South Bridgton. They also sold carriages. The photograph below, taken in 1933, is of Sylvester Bishop's grain store, another South Bridgton business.

NARRAMISSIC, THE PEABODY-FITCH FARM. For over a century, this South Bridgton farmhouse was lived in by descendants of William and Sally Peabody, who built it in 1797. It prospered throughout the first half of the 19th century. In 1850, the farm had 2 horses, 4 oxen, 12 dairy cows and cattle, 16 sheep, and a pig and produced corn, oats, peas, beans, potatoes, wool, beeswax, and honey. However, after the 1856 death of George Fitch, the Peabody's son-in-law, the farm's fortunes slowly deteriorated. In 1938, Margaret Monroe of Providence purchased it for use as a summer home, giving it the name Narramissic, which she understood to mean "hard to find." She bequeathed it to the Bridgton Historical Society in 1987. It is open during the summer for visitors to learn firsthand about 19th-century farm life.

NARRAMISSIC BARN AND BLACKSMITH SHOP. In 1829, Mary Peabody married George Fitch. He built an ell, and they shared the house she had grown up in with her parents, a fairly common practice at the time. In 1850, this was a fairly typical moderately prosperous inland Maine hill farm, with 80 acres of improved land and 120 acres of woodland. The family raised their own wheat, to be ground for flour, a practice that was becoming much less common in New England at the time. George also built the "Temperance Barn" (it was built without supplying the customary rum at the barn raising) and a workshop with a blacksmith forge. Thanks to Bob Dunning (below, left, who passed away unexpectedly in 2007), the historical society was able to restore the shop and forge to use for demonstrations and programs.

WORK HORSES AND OXEN, C. 1900. Before the advent of tractors and mechanized machinery, heavy farm work was accomplished by teams of horses or oxen. Charles C. Hamlin, of North Bridgton, had a fine team of horses (above). In the winter, he hauled timber, rising early in the morning to feed the horses before setting out for the logging site. Oxen, like the ones Sam Knight is shown with, were gradually replaced by horses for many tasks, as lighter and more efficiently designed plows and farm machinery became available during the 19th century. Even so, farming in Bridgton, as in much of northern New England, was an increasingly difficult undertaking, as the thin, hilly, rocky soil became depleted, making it difficult to compete with produce from the Midwest, with its flat, fertile land, easily worked by machinery.

HARVEST TIME ON HIGHLAND RIDGE. From left to right, Lola (Dodge) Gibbs, Daniel Wiggin, and Pamela Wiggin are seen here in front of bundles of corn stalks. Lola had married Benjamin (Ben) Gibbs in 1896, and their house stands in the background. Ben inherited a large sum of money from his mother's family, but unfortunately he did not inherit their business acumen, and sadly, both he and his wife died in poverty.

BRIGHAM FARM, MIDDLE RIDGE. This is a wonderful example of a connected farm, common throughout much of northern New England, with the house connected to the barn through a series of ells and outbuildings. As described by Thomas Hubka in *Big House, Little House, Back House, Barn*, this practice, adopted by reform-minded 19th-century farmers, created a south-facing dooryard where farm families could work, sheltered from the prevailing cold winter winds.

Three

THE LIFE OF THE MIND
EDUCATION, CULTURE, AND THE ARTS

BRIDGTON HIGH SCHOOL, 1875. Located on Gibbs Avenue, the town's first public high school cost $10,000 to construct in 1872. Flush toilets and electric lights were not installed until 1914. The building became the elementary school in 1949 when a new high school building was constructed on Depot Street. It was torn down in the 1990 after unsuccessful attempts by several groups to renovate and reuse it.

BRIDGTON ACADEMY. Samuel Andrews of North Bridgton, Enoch Perley of South Bridgton, and Dr. Samuel Farnsworth of the center spearheaded the establishment of Bridgton Academy, which incorporated in 1808 to provide area students with a secondary education. Controversy erupted over where it should be located, with North Bridgton winning out. Girls were admitted as early as 1833, although today it operates as the nation's only all-male postsecondary school.

SPRATT-MEAD MUSEUM, BRIDGTON ACADEMY. The Spratt-Mead Museum was opened in the early 1900s, although its origins date to earlier natural history collections. It is an eclectic mix of exotic ethnographic materials, natural history specimens, and historic artifacts, a true "Cabinet of Curiosities." The kayak hanging from the ceiling was donated in 1903. It is from Greenland, and said to have been used on one of Robert E. Peary's early arctic expeditions.

GIBBS AVENUE SCHOOL STUDENTS, 1880s. This is a photograph of students, perhaps the graduating class, at the Gibbs Avenue School, Bridgton's public high school. The high wheel bicycle probably received a lot of attention in Bridgton and may have been a source of pride for the owner. These bicycles first appeared in the United States around 1878 and were becoming popular among those who could afford them in the mid-1880s.

PRIMARY B SCHOOL. At one time, there were 22 separate neighborhood school districts in Bridgton. The largest was District No. 6 in the village. Two primary schools were built to serve the "scholars," as they were called. Primary A, was on north High Street, one of the town's more desirable residential neighborhoods, and this one, Primary B, was off lower Main Street, in a neighborhood dominated by mills and mill worker housing.

Bridgton High School Orchestra, 1928–1929. This photograph was in an album kept by Frances Webb, who graduated from Bridgton High School in 1931. According to a newspaper clipping that accompanies it, the orchestra was very highly thought of. It performed at numerous community and social events around town, in addition to school functions.

OLD PUBLIC LIBRARY. The public library was founded in 1895, although there had been earlier reading groups in town. It moved into this building in 1900. The library moved to its permanent location in 1913 when the Dalton Holmes Davis Public Library was constructed. In 1944, this building housed the Bridgton Business and Professional Women's Club, and it later became the Bridgton Hospital Guild thrift shop.

DALTON HOLMES DAVIS MEMORIAL, BRIDGTON, ME.

BRIDGTON PUBLIC LIBRARY. A bequest from Dalton Holmes Davis provided funds for the construction of a library building, which still serves the town. Listed on the National Register of Historic Places, the building has been renovated and expanded several times, most recently in 1997, when the Kendal and Anna Ham Memorial Wing, a two-story addition, was constructed in the rear of the building.

WALKER MEMORIAL HALL. Joseph Walker, a relative of the Gibbs family who lived on the Ridge, left $5,000 in his will to build a library, lecture hall, or facility for the promotion of agriculture. When Walker Hall was built in 1892, the view from the tower must have been much as it appears in the picture below. The hall was first used by the Ridge Literary Aid Society in 1893. Christmas parties, dances, and suppers were held there, and it had a small library. Dorothy Davis, whose family lived on the Ridge for generations, left a substantial amount of money in her will for the hall's restoration, and in 1992, it was rededicated to her. It is administered by trustees, and occasional lectures and programs are held at the hall during the summer months.

CHARLES LEWIS FOX.
Charles Fox, born in 1854, was an important, albeit often overlooked, Maine painter, active from around 1880 until his death in 1927. He trained at the Ecole des Beaux-Arts in Paris. In 1887, he opened a studio in Portland and advertised for students. He soon started inviting students and other artists to join him in Bridgton for the summer. His friend and fellow artist Curtis Perry (1854–1931), who had connections with the Flint family, may have influenced his decision to come to Bridgton. Fox was also active in the Socialist party, running for governor in 1902 and 1906. The cartoon below is from an autograph book in the Bridgton Historical Society collections. It must have been drawn in one of his first years in Bridgton.

May the marching Devil be
Always one days march from thee.

C.L.Fox
J.C.Barrett

Bridgton Sept 28th 1890

CHARLES FOX HOUSE. Charles Fox and Curtis Perry built this large symmetrical house on the upper ridge, reputedly designed to resemble Pleasant Mountain, which dominates the view. Most of the first floor rooms open onto a porch that faces the mountain. The two men were interested in music as well as the visual arts. During the early years of the 20th century, there were concerts and recitals for invited guests, held in a large upstairs room. Fox was also apparently something of a very early audiophile. He had the latest in phonographs and gave demonstrations of it to his friends. Writing in 1978, Cara Cook remembered visiting the house as a little girl. She described a mural depicting various mushroom species on the living room wall, and a manual elevator, which was raised by pulling hand over hand on a rope.

CHARLES FOX GARDENS. In his book on the history of North Bridgton, Guy Monk described seeing Fox and Perry about town, an inseparable but unlikely pair. Fox was tall and lanky next to the much shorter Perry, although both dressed casually in shirt, trousers, and sandals. Occasionally they wore sun helmets but usually went hatless. They also established these impressive gardens above their house. They discovered a ledge in Waterford with an unusual mix of granite and other minerals and hired someone to blast the ledge and haul the tons of rock the six miles to their house with horses. One large rock, which stood in the middle about eight feet high, required 12 yokes of oxen to move. The elaborate stonework and spectacular plantings attracted many admiring visitors. Sadly for unknown reasons, at some point, the two friends quarreled and never reconciled.

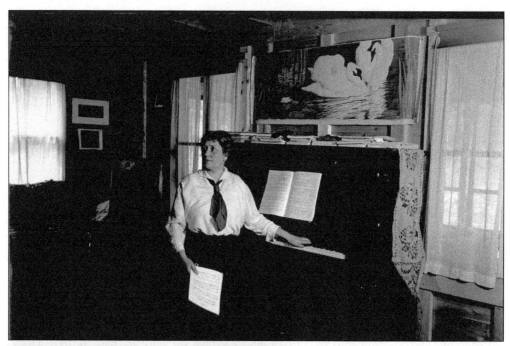

OLIVE FREMSTAD, METROPOLITAN OPERA STAR. In 1914, Olive Fremstad, one of the premier sopranos of the early 20th century, purchased a lot on the shore of Highland Lake and built an elaborate summer home, which she called Nawandyn. Her neighbors had unusual opportunities to meet celebrities of the day when some of her well-known friends came to visit. She and other nationally known stars also performed at the Saco Valley Music Festival, which was held each year during this period at the town hall, under the direction of L. B. Cain. These photographs illustrate that the sophisticated cosmopolitan diva had an unexpected taste for the outdoors country life.

MUSIC ROOM OF NAWANDYN. This is a wonderful image of a well-appointed interior from the early 20th century. Fremstad was married to Harry Lewis Brainard in this room on November 4, 1916. She sold the house in 1926, and the Darneille family used it for many years as a summer home.

MARIE SUNDELIUS. Another famous opera star with local connections, Marie Sundelius studied with Frederick Bristol, a highly respected music teacher from New York who summered in Harrison, bringing many of his pupils with him. The *History of Harrison* described her as "one of the most beloved of the summer residents of Harrison." She performed at the Saco Valley Music Festival at the town hall in 1914, when she autographed this picture.

RUFUS PORTER MUSEUM. Rufus Porter (1792–1894) spent much of his childhood in the Bridgton area. He was a well-known itinerant artist and muralist, traveling throughout New England, New York, and as far south as Virginia. He is best known for the large landscape murals he painted on plaster walls. Porter, who founded *Scientific American* magazine, had an extremely fertile, inventive mind. He took out over 100 patents, including a design for an airship, and he sold a design for a revolving rifle to Samuel Colt for $100, indicative of his inability to capitalize financially on his inventions. He painted murals in a number of houses in and around Bridgton, including this house on South High Street that is now the Rufus Porter Museum, devoted to Porter's work and carrying on his legacy of teaching the arts. (Courtesy Rufus Porter Museum.)

MABEL POTTER WITH HER QUILT, 1928. Mabel Potter lived on Highland Ridge. Like many women of her day, she appears to have been a talented needleworker, as another photograph shows her inside her house working on a braided rug. A notation on the back of this photograph reads "Taken Sept 1928. Size seven feet by four feet. For her twin from Mabel."

CAST OF UNKNOWN PLAY, 1899. Amateur theatricals were very popular in Bridgton. The actors pictured here are, from left to right, (first row) Willie E. Ingalls, Charles Marshall, and Alice Palmer Ingalls; (second row) Liston Ingalls, George Smith, and Elizabeth Staley Ingalls. The third row includes Forrest Abbott, Lizzie Crosley Abbot, Ed Weston, Harry Kingman, Jeanne Whitney Smith, and Walter Abbot.

GIBBS HALL OR THE OPERA HOUSE. This building, built in 1867, housed businesses on the first floor and a hall on the second floor where school programs and other performances were held. When Perley P. Burnham started his business here, it was the first store in this part of Maine that sold only dry goods, and the business prospered until Burnham's death in 1929. School entertainments, programs, exhibitions of the early agricultural fairs, and fairs like this one (below) to benefit the public library were held in the hall upstairs. It was here, in 1913, that the first moving pictures to be seen in Bridgton were shown. It stood at "the fork," now the middle of Main Street above Shorey Park. Gibbs Mill is visible in the background of the photograph above.

TIMOTHY'S QUEST. In 1922, the silent movie *Timothy's Quest* was filmed at various local venues, including the Farnsworth-Decker House in North Bridgton (below). Based on a book by Kate Douglas Wiggin, it tells the story of two children who run away from an orphanage to look for a mother. Timothy (one of the orphans) was played by Joseph Depew, who grew up to direct *The Beverly Hillbillies*. This was not the only Hollywood movie with Bridgton connections. Stephen King, a part-time resident of Lovell, is said to have based scenes from *The Mist* and other works in Bridgton, and in 1977, he arranged to have the world premiere of *The Shining* at the Magic Lantern Theater. The War Tax was a 1 percent sales tax to pay for the debt from World War I.

MAGIC LANTERN THEATER. By 1929, the old tannery building was deteriorating, and Claude Meserve replaced it with a garage and automobile showroom on the first floor and, much like the opera house and other buildings with auditoriums and halls, a theater on the second floor. Known first as Meserve's Theater, it was later operated as the Mayfair, and finally as the Magic Lantern Theater. Unfortunately the building's foundation rested on wet and unstable ground, and by 2007, there was no feasible alternative to tearing it down. In 2008, the new Magic Lantern Theater, owned by Down East Enterprises, opened here, set back somewhat from its original location. The state-of-the-art facility boasts three separate theaters, one with a stage, and the Tannery Pub, which shows art films and hosts musical acts and local group activities.

STATE THEATER. The State Theater was built by Eugene Tenney in 1935 at the corner of Main and Elm Streets. It replaced public tennis courts, which were on the earlier site of the corn-packing plant. Clarence "Dutch" Millet, who had come to town to mange the Brookside Theater, was the first manager of the State Theater. By the late 1960s, it was experiencing financial difficulties, in part as a result of competition from television. On Monday, March 24, 1969, passers-by reported hearing creaking and groaning sounds coming from the building. The roof collapsed that evening from a very heavy snow load. (Below, photograph by Al Glover, courtesy Bridgton Historical Society.)

NORTON'S ORCHESTRA. Norton's Orchestra was a popular musical group in Bridgton during the 1920s. It traveled from Maine to Florida by train and steamboat, stopping to play in various towns along the way. One night in Georgia, they played "Marching through Georgia," not realizing that it was about William Tecumseh Sherman's march to the sea in the Civil War, when he burned everything in sight, and the crowd stormed the stage and chased them out.

THE BOSTONIANS. According to a notation on the back of this photograph, the Bostonians were another musical group that came to Bridgton every year to perform. This picture was taken by the side of the Cumberland House hotel on Main Street.

BRIDGTON BAND. The first band in town was organized in 1851. Following the Civil War, two competing bands were formed, but in 1882, they once again joined forces. Several different bands came and went in the ensuing decades. This is an early photograph of the Bridgton Band, apparently taken either before or after a parade. The Methodist church on Main Street is visible in the background.

MODERN WOODMEN BAND. The Modern Woodmen of America Camp 10269, a fraternal organization, was organized in 1901. The Modern Woodmen Band was started in 1905 and was in existence until 1921. Frank Cash was the band's director, and Frank Webb was the manager. They met in several different locations during their existence, so it is unclear where they posed for this amusing photograph.

THE BRIDGTON BAND AND BANDSTAND. The photograph above, taken in the early 1990s, shows the Bridgton Band at the railroad station. The reason for the cowboy hats has been lost to history. The most recent version of the band, the Bridgton Community Band, was formed in 1938 and is still going strong. The original bandstand was built in 1863 at the top of Main Hill (below). It was also used as a dais for speakers at political events, and moved several times, to Post Office Square, and then to Highland Lake. The present bandstand occupies a site near Stevens Brook Elementary School, but at this writing it may be moved once again.

Four

FUN IN THE SUN
OUTDOOR RECREATION AND TOURISM

PLEASANT MOUNTAIN AND MOOSE POND. With 10 lakes and ponds, forests, parks, and a ski area, Bridgton has something for everyone who loves the outdoors. This photograph was taken from the causeway, probably around 1900. Today much of Pleasant Mountain is Shawnee Peak ski area. The first rope tow on the mountain was built in 1938, making this the longest continually operating ski area in the state.

PLEASANT MOUNTAIN HOUSE. In June 1850, a two-story hotel with a bowling alley was opened on top of Pleasant Mountain. Visitors were transported by horse-drawn carriage to the foot of the mountain, where they had the choice of either walking or riding up the carriage road. The original hotel burned around 1860 and was replaced in 1872 by Charles E. Gibbs, who purchased the property and built another large structure with 26 rooms. Over 300 attended the grand opening on July 4, 1873, enjoying the music of Carter's Band from Boston and the spectacular view from the porch. The hotel was closed for most of the 1880s and 1890s, but reopened in 1901, renovated completely and equipped with a telephone. Unfortunately vandalism and the high cost of doing business made it an unprofitable operation, and in 1908, it was sold to John Pike, who tore it down for the lumber, which he used to build his farm in East Fryeburg. In 1920, the fire tower was built on this site.

COTTAGES, INGALLS GROVE.
During the 19th century, Owen
Ingalls leased land on the shore
of Highland Lake to families
from New York and southern
New England, who stayed in
tents to enjoy fishing and other
outdoor recreational activities.
Some liked the area so well that
they signed 100-year leases and
built their own cottages. The
group below is relaxing at Old
Point Comfort, which, judging by
the woman in the hammock and
the begging dog, appears to have
been aptly named. The woman
in front to the "Boats to Let"
sign is identified as "Aunt Emma
Larrabee," and there appears to
be an observation deck of some
sort on top of the roof.

INTERIOR OF INGALLS GROVE COTTAGE. These cottages, although rustic, clearly provided a more comfortable environment for vacationers than the tents they first used. Later in the 20th century, descendants of some of the families who originally built these cottages were still using them, and when Owen Ingalls's grandson Andrew Sanborn inherited the leases, he made it possible for them to buy the land their cottages stood on.

"SHADY SHORE" COTTAGE. This simple cottage is on Highland Lake, one of at least 10 lakes and ponds located at least partly in Bridgton. According to a notation on the back of this photograph, the gentleman on the left is Jesse Frisbie, and his wife sits across from him. The woman in front is unidentified. Frisbie ran a marble and gravestone shop in town.

LONG LAKE LODGE, NORTH BRIDGTON, C. 1905. Long Lake Lodge was a school for boys preparing for college, opened in the early years of the 20th century by former Bridgton Academy teacher E. V. Spooner. Interestingly this is very similar to the current mission of Bridgton Academy, which is a postsecondary school for boys. Long Lake Lodge was originally located in the boathouse pictured below. The boys slept in tents, and meals were served in the Bridgton Academy dining room. Although the lodge was more of a summer school or early camp, the tents pictured here are good illustrations of those used at the time by families and sportsmen who wanted to experience the Maine woods.

Long Lake Lodge, North Bridgton, Maine.

THE BRIDGTON HOUSE, C. 1880S. This location, at the top of Main Hill, has a long history as part of Bridgton's hospitality industry. In 1789, the Sears Tavern was opened across the street. After that property burned in the 1830s, Richard Gage Sr. acquired the house on the site that would eventually become the Bridgton House. He enlarged it and opened Gage's Tavern. He also lived in the house. In 1860, Mial Davis purchased the property. At various times, he leased it to others, but following the Civil War, he enlarged it and took over the management himself. It was operated as the Davis Hotel and later the Bridgton House. It was during this period that it had the distinctive three-story porch, as can be seen in this early photograph of the Bridgton Band. A fire in 1896 destroyed much of this hotel.

THE BRIDGTON HOUSE, C. 1899. This photograph was evidently taken soon after the hotel was rebuilt following the 1896 fire. This building, with its broad wraparound porch, was designed by noted Portland architect John Calvin Stevens. By this time, it was operated by Charles E. Cobb and George Cabot. The new hotel had four full floors and a basement, and with 74 rooms, it was much larger than the building it replaced. The hotel also boasted running water and was considered to be a rather luxurious establishment in those early years of the 20th century. In 1914, fire again damaged the hotel. A fire broke out near the top of the building while the manager, who was then Mrs. Stephen Winslow, was burning trash in the fireplace. There was not enough water pressure to reach that high, and the building burned to the first story. In 1915, Howard Burnham bought the property and salvaged what was left of the building. For many years, it was used as a private residence, but is now operated as a bed-and-breakfast.

THE HOTEL CUMBERLAND. The photograph above was taken after 1888, when a third story was added, following the death of Marshall Bacon. Bacon had transformed what was originally the home of Rufus Chase into a hotel in 1858. The hotel had a livery stable in the back, and its team of horses met trains arriving at the railroad station to take them to the hotel and other local destinations. The sad end of the Cumberland hotel came on November 17, 1970, when it was torn down. In 1978, a Dairy Queen was opened on this lot, which is on the corner of Bacon and Main Streets. A succession of businesses followed, and in 2008, Chalmers Insurance Group opened a claims center here.

LAKE VIEW HOUSE, C. 1935. The Lake View House, operated by A. L. Burnham, was listed as a house for summer boarders in 1897. It is unlikely that a sign welcoming "transients" would be considered good marketing today. However, it does suggest that by the time this photograph was taken, there were more travelers looking for a place to stay one night, as opposed to those staying for several weeks or more on an extended vacation.

LADY OF THE LAKE. This small steamer ran two daily sightseeing excursions around Highland Lake. The two-hour trip cost 25¢. A second boat, the *Highland Laddie*, could be towed behind if there were too many passengers for the *Lady of the Lake*. Many of the cottages kept horns handy to signal a greeting to the boat as she passed by, and the boat would return the greeting by sounding her own horn.

HIGHLAND LAKE REGATTA. These photographs show a huge summer celebration at the foot of Highland Lake. The double boathouse on the opposite shore is at Shorey Grove, which is directly across from the current town beach and boat landing. These photographs, identified on the back as being part of Old Home Days, were probably taken in 1914. The foot of Highland Lake is just a block from Main Street. Bridgton has the unusual and fortunate distinction of having a town beach practically in the center of town.

WATER BASEBALL AT LONG LAKE. This old postcard shows an unusual form of water sport at one of the many children's camps in town. Summer camps first became popular around the beginning of the 20th century, as middle- and upper-class city dwellers decided that fresh air and wholesome country activities would make their children healthier in body and mind.

OUR WOODLANDS SHORE, CAMP WOODLANDS, BRIDGTON, ME

CAMP WOODLANDS. Camp Woodlands was located on Long Lake, off the Kansas Road. According to the 1925 *Handbook for Summer Camps* by Porter Sargent, Camp Woodlands was "a summer camp for Jewish girls." It was founded by Rachel Shwartz, who purchased the property from the Winslow family. Fires destroyed two buildings, one in 1973 and the other in 1977. It closed in the early 1980s, and fire destroyed the main house in 1986.

VACATION COTTAGE. This cottage was built for Herbert L. Smith on a hilltop in the Hio Ridge neighborhood in the western portion of Bridgton. Smith later moved it to Sabatis Island on the Moose Pond Causeway, where it was rented for recreational purposes. The cottage was torn down in the 1940s, and the lumber was used to enlarge the gift shop that Smith and his wife, Marjorie, ran on the island. This little girl, identified only by her initials, M. L. S., was probably a member of the Steadman family. She is pictured on the porch of the cottage.

SABATIS ISLAND GIFT SHOP, MOOSE POND CAUSEWAY. Herbert and Marjorie Smith rented cottages and ran a gift shop here for a number of years. In 1919, the Smiths started taking in boarders, gradually replacing the original tents with cottages. In 1968, Marjorie stopped renting cottages, and she closed the gift shop in 1969. Today the cottages are gone, but the 15-acre island is a town-owned picnic area.

BENJAMIN GIBBS AND FRIEND, EARLY 20TH CENTURY. Locals enjoy outdoor sports and recreation as much as tourists "from away" enjoy them. The man on the right in this photograph is Benjamin Walker Gibbs, who lived on a farm on Highland Ridge. The other man has not been fully identified, but according to a note with the photograph, his last name was Burgess. These fish were probably caught on nearby Highland Lake.

ICE FISHING HOUSE, C. 1900. This is a photograph, seen from left to right above, of Idalyn M. Gove Staples; her husband, Winburn Staples; and an unidentified man. These were probably taken on Highland Lake. Winburn was a successful banker and businessman who served in the state legislature and was instrumental in bringing electricity to Bridgton, and the Staples were able to enjoy the sport of ice fishing with a degree of comfort. Although today the horse has been replaced by pick-up trucks or snowmobiles, with a heater and a rather fancy-looking dining room chair, this ice fishing shack (or "winter fishing cabin," as the back of the photograph above puts it) has many of the amenities of ice fishing houses so common on today's frozen lakes and ponds.

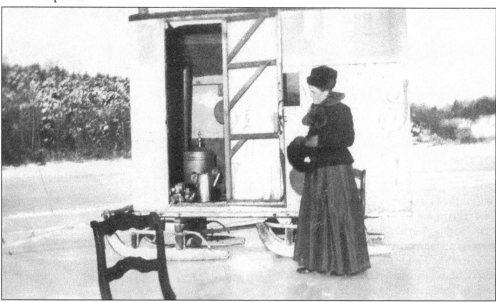

Five

LIVING TOGETHER
SOME NOTABLE PEOPLE, COMMUNITY
ORGANIZATIONS, AND EVENTS

PARADE IN POST OFFICE SQUARE. This photograph from the 1930s was taken from the top floor of the Knights of Pythias Block (now Reny's Department Store). The large turnout and festive atmosphere attest to the popularity of the Fourth of July parades that have been a fixture in Bridgton for many years.

THE FOURTH OF JULY PARADE. These pictures were taken during even earlier Fourth of July parades, probably around 1900. The photograph above was taken on Depot Street (the tannery building is visible in the background). It is the float of Charles Wentworth, who was a blacksmith, and he can be seen swinging his hammer. The driver is Charles Artie Gibbs, also from Bridgton. The photograph below was taken during the same era on South High Street. Local businesses and groups entered floats in the parade, much as they do today. This float was from Frank Gibbs, who sold home furnishings from his store in Pondicherry Square.

DEDICATION OF THE SOLDIERS MONUMENT, JULY 21, 1910. Henry B. Cleaves, governor of Maine from 1892 to 1896, donated a 36-foot-tall monument to his native town in 1910, commemorating the 200 Bridgton men who served the Union cause in the Civil War and the 36 who died during that conflict. A crowd of 3,000 attended the dedication ceremony for the monument, which stills stands at the top of Main Hill. Four panels decorate the base of the monument, dedicating it "In Honor of the Living: In Grateful Memory of the Dead. To Bridgton's Sons who defended the Union, 1861–1865. They Strove That The Nation Might Live: That Government Of The People, By The People, For The People, Should Not Perish. One Country, One Destiny, One Flag."

BRIDGTON MEMBERS OF THE 30TH INFANTRY REGIMENTAL BAND. This is a photograph of, from left to right, Isaiah Webb, Edward C. Webb, Osgood Webb, and Walter Webb, all from Bridgton, in camp during the Civil War. Col. James Webb and all seven of his sons enlisted in the Union army. In fact, one of them, John Tyler Webb, was the first from Bridgton to enlist. He was far from alone though; when Pres. Abraham Lincoln issued a call for volunteers in 1861, 200 men from Bridgton responded to the appeal. Many of the town's future leaders took part in the Civil War, and the list of those from Bridgton who enlisted and served is a long one and is one that includes men from every walk of life, from future Maine governor Henry B. Cleaves to Edwin C. Milliken who, at the age of 13, was the youngest Bridgton resident to enlist.

REUNION OF THE 15TH MAINE REGIMENT. This is a reunion of Maj. Henry Shorey's unit. Shorey, who moved to Bridgton after the war and founded the *Bridgton News*, enlisted from Bath in 1861, rose through the ranks to captain and was mustered out in 1866. Later he wrote a history of the 15th Maine Regiment. Major Shorey and his daughter Eva Shorey are standing to the left of the gentleman in the chair, Col. Isaac Dyer.

GRAND ARMY OF THE REPUBLIC (GAR) ON MAIN STREET. The GAR, formed in 1866 in Illinois, was an organization of Union Civil War veterans. Nationally the GAR was very influential, credited with establishing Memorial Day as a remembrance of fallen servicemen (and now women). In 1928, when all the Civil War veterans had passed away, a Farragut Memorial Association was formed to continue the mission in Bridgton.

BRIDGTON CANNING CENTER. From 1943 to 1945, the Bridgton Canning Center operated in the home economics classroom of the high school, canning fruits and vegetables from local victory gardens. It was one of 50 such centers in the state of Maine. A paid director and assistant were helped by volunteers who canned the produce that gardeners brought in. In exchange for this service, the center kept one out of every five cans for the school lunch program, community welfare, or disaster relief. Some simply donated their produce outright. In 1944, the center put up 4,785 cans of various kinds of vegetables, fruits, and chicken. Pictured below are, from left to right, Blanche Bennet, Fannie Ingalls, Stella Cole, Irene Meserve, Clithero Pearson, and Elsa Swanson.

PREPARING CORN FOR CANNING. Obviously there were a few men who volunteered along with the ladies at the canning center. Here Clayton Sanborn is operating a hand-cranked device to shell corn. The ladies husking the corn are, from left to right, Alice Dunn, Grace Widdows, and Irene Meserve, who was the center's leader.

RED CROSS LADIES, 1943. This is a group of Red Cross volunteers, photographed at the public library in 1943. During World War II, the Red Cross supplied instructions for knitting blankets, socks, and other supplies needed for the war effort. This was just one of the many ways that the men and women of Bridgton supported the war effort.

Horse-Drawn Fire Engine. Fires played a major role in the history of Bridgton's development, and in the days before modern equipment, they posed an even greater danger than they do today. In 1873, a devastating fire spurred interest in establishing a fire department. Eighty-two men volunteered for the department, the town voted to purchase a Babcock Fire Extinguisher and a Boston Hunneman tub and constructed a reservoir.

Steam Fire Engine "The Bridgton," 1889. This is one of two early fire engines used in Bridgton, the other one being called "the Victor." This engine, fighting a fire at the Trumble house across the brook from the tannery, was pulled by a pair of chestnut horses owned by Charles "Artie" Gibbs. The two firemen are George "Duffer" Knight (left) and Win Phinney.

"DIAMOND T" FIRE TRUCK, 1939. This is a photograph of the Bridgton Fire Department members in action using their "Diamond T" fire truck, which was brand new at the time. The first attempt to establish a fire department had come in 1854, when the Bridgton Centre Fire Corporation was incorporated to serve the central village area. The corporation had the authority to elect officers, purchase equipment, construct a building, and incur any other necessary expenses, which were to be paid by a special tax. They built a firehouse for $450 and purchased firefighting equipment. The equipment proved to be useless, and the effort fell by the wayside until the fire of 1873 spurred the town to action. A firehouse was built in 1878, and the first alarm system was installed in 1906. The department, with stations in South Bridgton/Sandy Creek, North Bridgton, and West Bridgton, is dependent on dedicated members who are on call and ready to protect the lives and property of Bridgton citizens.

Going to the
Bridgton Fair,
Sept. 24, 25, 26, 1907.

THE BRIDGTON AGRICULTURAL FAIR. The earliest Bridgton Fairs were joint ventures with the nearby town of Harrison, but the two towns quickly went their own way. The Bridgton Farmers and Mechanics Club held its first fair in 1884. Livestock was exhibited in the field by the town hall on North High Street, agricultural equipment inside the town hall, and the "Ladies Exhibits" were in nearby Gibbs Hall. In 1892, it moved to the west side of South High Street (the present site of the hospital). The fairgrounds eventually included a two-story exhibition hall, trotting track, and grandstand. In 1914, the Bridgton Agricultural Society was formed, supplanting the Farmers and Mechanics Club. The three-day fair continued to be a big attraction into the 1920s, but interest waned in the 1930s, and it was discontinued.

"To Highland Grange, a Fair Prize." Highland Grange No. 116 in Bridgton was organized in 1875 and lasted until 1964. These are apparently some of the products displayed at the Bridgton Agricultural Fair. Interest in the fair lagged in the 1920s, and in the 1930s, the federal government took over the fairgrounds to build a Civilian Conservation Corps (CCC) camp.

Town Hall. This building replaced the original town hall, which stood opposite the cemetery on South High Street. The 1852 dedication address by Marshall Cram was the first history of the town. Originally with a symmetrical double-door entrance, the building was renovated in 1902, creating the facade seen here. It now houses a gymnasium, and elections, meetings, and programs are held here, but the town offices are on Chase Street.

ENOCH PERLEY HOUSE. This is the first house that Enoch Perley built in South Bridgton (it was later moved to the foot of Highland Lake). Perley, son of one of the proprietors, moved to Bridgton in 1765 from Boxford, Massachusetts. The Perleys became one of Bridgton's dominant families in those early years. They owned more than 2,000 acres of timberland in the state. Enoch died in 1829 at 80.

LT. ROBERT ANDREWS HOUSE. Bunker Hill veteran Robert Andrews settled in South Bridgton in 1780, living alone while he cleared farmland. He eventually added an ell so to house a family to help manage the farm. The Cleaves family lived here for a while, and future governor Henry B. Cleaves was born here. Andrews was generous and kind and established a fund to help the "worthy and industrious poor."

JOHN PEABODY HOUSE. This house was built by Deacon John Peabody and Mary (Perley) Peabody, parents of William Peabody, who built the Bridgton Historical Society's Narramissic. John served in military campaigns against the French and Native Americans and in a militia company that marched on Bunker Hill. The Peabodys moved to Bridgton during the winter of 1783–1784. The First Congregational Church of Bridgton was founded in this house in 1784.

FIRST CONGREGATIONAL CHURCH. The provision of a minister and church was an integral part of the original land grant from Massachusetts. In 1788, the appropriately named Nathan Church, related to both the Perleys and the Peabodys, became the first minister. A meetinghouse, which also served municipal functions, was built in 1791. In 1833, a church was built, but in 1870, that building was replaced by this one, which still stands.

SOUTH BRIDGTON CONGREGATIONAL CHURCH. As the population of the town increased, a second parish in South Bridgton seemed desirable and was established in 1829. The congregation met in this meetinghouse for many years, but a Gothic-style church building was constructed to replace it in 1871. In 1832, yet another parish was established in North Bridgton.

BAPTIST CHURCH, NORTH HIGH STREET. This building, constructed in 1815, was substantially remodeled in 1832 and 1851. Its distinctive weather vane is now in the collection of the Bridgton Historical Society. This photograph was taken in 1902 just before it was torn down to make way for Farragut Memorial Park. Forrest Abbott disassembled the building and rebuilt it as a barn on his farm on the Ridge, where it stands today.

METHODIST CHURCH. Construction of this building began in 1869 but was not completed until December 1871. The financial difficulties that caused this delay may have been partly due to the fact that three other churches in town were also erecting new buildings at that time, stretching local benefactors' resources. St. Peter's Episcopal Church shared this building for a number of years, but work on a new Episcopal church is now complete.

UNIVERSALIST CHURCH. The Universalist Society in Bridgton dates to 1839, but this building was constructed in 1870. In 1924, St. Joseph's Catholic Church acquired it, an important step for them in a largely Protestant town. To discourage violent disruption, three prominent masons had been asked to attend the first mass in town in 1913. The Catholic church is now on South High Street, and this building is Craftworks, a boutique.

THE NORTHERN CUMBERLAND MEMORIAL HOSPITAL. This house on Main Hill was built in 1870 and later remodeled (as shown here). In 1917, Dr. Edward Abbott began raising funds to establish a hospital, which eventually opened in this house. It served as the town's hospital until 1964, when a new building was constructed on South High Street. This building is now Favorite Part-times Antiques, run by Brandon and Deborah Woolley.

THE HOSPITAL. In 1945, Freeman Curtis left the hospital $30,000 in his will. This formed the nucleus of a fund-raising campaign designed to raise $100,000 for the construction of a new building, which was to serve 15 towns. During the 1950s, improvements were made at the old hospital, with the purchase of an X-ray machine and other equipment. Finally in 1963, enough money was raised ($200,000 by that time) to construct a new building (above). It served the Lakes Region well for many years, but in the late 1990s, it again became clear that new facilities were needed, and the new hospital, below, was opened in 2002. The name was changed to Bridgton Hospital, it became part of the Central Maine Medical Family, and Bridgton has continued to serve the medical needs of the area.

The Bridgton News

Established 1870

The Oldest Continuous Business Now In Existence
In Bridgton With Ownership In One Family

Major Henry A. Shorey
Founder
Editor & Publisher
1870-1923

Henry A. (Harry) Shorey Jr.
Editor & Publisher
1923-1952

Henry A. Shorey III
Publisher
Since 1952

Congratulations To Our Town On Its 200th Birthday!

It has been a pleasure to serve this friendly community
as its news and advertising media for 98 years.

May BRIDGTON GROW AND PROSPER In The Years Ahead!

THE BRIDGTON NEWS. The *Bridgton News* was founded in 1870 by Maj. Henry A. Shorey, who moved to Bridgton from Bath after serving in the Civil War. The newspaper moved into the building above in 1879. Originally there was a blacksmith shop on the first floor, and A. B. Pratt manufactured carriages on the second floor. Eva Shorey, daughter of the paper's editor, Major Shorey, is the woman seated on the right, and Charles Stickney, a reporter and Bridgton historian, is the man standing in the center. The other people's identities are not known. The advertisement for the newspaper, at left, comes from the program for the town's celebration of its bicentennial in 1968. The three generations of Shoreys shown in the advertisement have now been succeeded by a fourth, Stephen Shorey, the son of Henry A. Shorey III.

MR. AND MRS. HENRY A. SHOREY III. Eula Shorey took over as managing editor of the newspaper in 1956 when Henry became Bridgton postmaster. She was the 1981 Maine Press Association Journalist of the Year. She has also found time to lead a very active community life and raise a family. She is a charter member of the Bridgton Historical Society and has attended every annual meeting since its founding in 1953.

BRIDGTON STAR NEWSPAPER STAFF. Although the *Bridgton News* has been the town's newspaper since 1870, it has not always been the only newspaper. Shortly after World War II, Ed Decker established another weekly, the *Bridgton Star*. After about six unprofitable months, he sold it to Robert Dingley and his wife, but the *Bridgton Star* ceased publication after another year or so. Seen here are, from left to right, Robert Dingley, Helen Dingley, and Barbara Graffam (Hemeon).

BRIDGTON LITERARY CLUB. The Bridgton Literary Club was founded in 1909, largely due to the energy of Clara Staples, its first president. Its original purpose was historical research. The club undertook a number of civic projects supporting, among other causes, students, the library, and the hospital. The club won a Sears-Roebuck Foundation prize in 1959 for its Welcoming Newcomers project, which helped new town residents feel more at home.

THE BUSINESS AND PROFESSIONAL WOMEN'S CLUB OF BRIDGTON. Part of an international organization, the Bridgton chapter of the Business and Professional Women's Club (BPW) was founded in 1923 with about 50 members. Its motto was "Better business women for a better world." It was involved with many community projects, particularly those involving activities for young people.

DEDICATION OF "TREES," 1934. Walter Hawkins and his wife, Annie Gallison, lived here during the summer. Hawkins worked at Jordan Marsh in Boston. The couple were very socially active in Bridgton and generous benefactors for the hospital and other causes. The story goes that when he turned off Main Street, the sound of the car horn playing "How Dry I Am," alerted the household to get his cocktail ready.

"ARNIE" ALLEN (LEFT) AND WALTER HAWKINS, 1930s. "Arnie" Allen was a popular local character, often seen with his beloved dog. A "severe shock" left him impaired. Wanting to stand on his own two feet, he managed to make a living. He lived in what was described as a "camp" on Nulty Street. When it burned, townspeople chipped in to buy an old carpenter shop on Depot Street for him to live in.

CCC Camp. The CCC, established in 1933, was a work and relief program that provided young men from unemployed families with work on conservation projects in rural areas. They worked 40 hours a week and received $30 per month, out of which they were required to send at least $25 home. The Bridgton Camp, the 1124th Company, included over 20 buildings.

CCC Sign and Workers. This sign was apparently erected at one of the local projects. Nationally workers performed a variety of jobs, constructing park buildings, trails, logging and fire roads, installing telephone and power lines, and performing other such tasks. The local camp helped to build the first ski trail at Pleasant Mountain. The first rope tow was built in 1938, and Bridgton became a popular destination for winter sport enthusiasts.

WINTER CARNIVAL PROGRAM COVER, 1941. In 1940, 6,000 people attended the first Bridgton Winter Carnival, which included skating, ski races, tobogganing, sled dog races, ice and snow sculptures, a ball, a parade, and other activities. The 1941 carnival also featured the first Interscholastic Winter Sports meet. Schools within 25 miles of Bridgton were invited to participate in events that included snowshoe, skating, and ski races. That year the New England Skating Association also sanctioned a speed skating championship in a specially constructed arena at Walker's Cove. But the event that attracted the most attention was the largest bobsled in the world, dubbed the "Miss Maine," which was 76 feet long and carried 113 people down Dodge's Hill and across to Highland Lake. Those at the very back were usually thrown off at the last curve, although none were seriously hurt. In recent years, the Musher's Bowl sled dog races have sparked a revival of this event.

THE WINTER SPORTS QUEEN AND HER COURT, 1941. Each year a queen of the carnival was crowned. This photograph shows the queen Marion Knight and her court on the elaborate ice throne constructed by A. K. Thorndike and Stanley Kramer (who owned Kramer's Ice House) on Highland Lake. In a coronation described as "spectacular," the queen was heralded by trumpeters, drummers, torchbearers, four ladies-in-waiting, and the 1940 queen, Betty Mabry.

WINTER CARNIVAL GIFTS. Merchants participated in the carnival festivities and no doubt profited from the thousands who visited town. The window of this unidentified store is loaded with gifts for the carnival queen and her ladies-in-waiting. Other store windows displayed some of the latest in winter sports equipment and fashions, to be given away in a prize drawing.

WINTER CARNIVAL PARADE, 1941. The huge crowd lining Main Street in Post Office Square attests to the popularity of this event in the 1940s. The sled dogs pictured here may have taken part in the 15-mile races, sanctioned by the New England Sled Dog Association, which started and finished at the Winter Sports Area at Highland Lake.

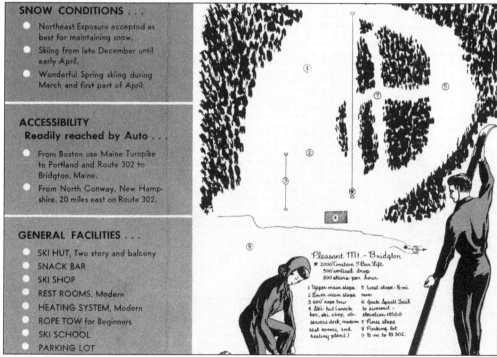

PLEASANT MOUNTAIN SKI AREA BROCHURE. The ski area has grown considerably since this brochure was produced. In 1988, 50 years after the first trail was established, a Pennsylvania group purchased the property and renamed it Shawnee Peak. They expanded the lodge and the amount of terrain for beginners, installed a new chairlift and lights for night skiing, and it became the largest night-skiing area in New England.

BRIDGTON RED SOX BASEBALL PLAYERS. Bridgton had active town baseball teams in the first half of the 20th century. Here Bridgton Red Sox catcher Carl Kilborn and shortstop Phil Richards (on the right) congratulate pitcher Harold Conant for his 2-1 victory over South Portland in their last game.

BRIDGTON HIGH SCHOOL BASEBALL TEAM, 1908. Only a few of the members of this team from a century ago can be identified. Clarence Libby is in the middle of the first row, Maurice Hamblen (not in uniform) is on the left in the second row, next to Edward Smith, and in the third row, the figure in the middle with the grin is identified as Dr. Richard March.

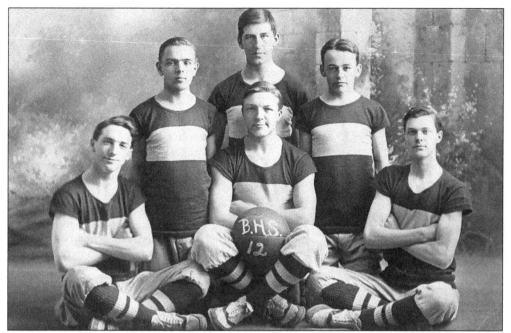

BRIDGTON HIGH SCHOOL BOYS BASKETBALL TEAM, 1912. The members of this long-ago team are, from left to right, (first row) Albert Norton, Walter Douglass, and Clifton Leach; (second row) Ray Larrabee, Fred Marriner, and Arthur Riley.

BRIDGTON HIGH SCHOOL GIRLS BASKETBALL TEAM, 1912. Although it is hard to imagine playing basketball in these uniforms, girls did have some opportunities to participate in high school sports. Members of this team are, from left to right, (first row) Beulah Towne, Addie Gore, Mildred Arey, Grace Burnham, and Edna Willby; (second row) Margory Davis, Winnie Arey, and Charlotte Abbott.

BRIDGTON HISTORICAL SOCIETY MUSEUM. In 1976, the town gave the old fire station, which is adjacent to the former site of the high school, to the Bridgton Historical Society to use as its first permanent headquarters. Previously the group used a room in the basement of the library. The building's tower was used to hang and dry the hoses when the engines returned following a fire. Historical society members shown at the door of their new facility are, from left to right, Claude Meserve, Irene Meserve, Mrs. Ray Whitney, Ray Whitney, Irving Linscott, Burton Mabry, Mildred Plunkett, and Dorothy Davis. In 1994, the society built an addition on the left-hand side of the building to house its library and archives.

BIBLIOGRAPHY

Blake, Judith L. *Rediscovering Bridgton's Main Street*. Bridgton, ME: Bridgton Historical Society, 2004.

Bridgton Historical Society. *Bridgton, Maine, 1768–1994*. Bridgton, ME: Bridgton Historical Society, 1993.

Brockett, Erik R. "Charles Lewis Fox (1854–1927): Early Maine Modernist and Regionalist." Undergraduate thesis, Harvard University, 1996.

Davis, Blynn Edwin. *The Ridge*. Bridgton, ME: self-published, 1971.

Eastman, Joel, and Paul E. Rivard. "Transportation and Manufacturing." *Maine: The Pine Tree State from Prehistory to the Present*. Richard W. Judd, Edwin A. Churchill, Joel W. Eastman, eds. Orono, ME: University of Maine Press, 1995.

Holden, Theodore L., and Russel W. Knight. *The Songo River Steamboats*. Salem, MA: American Neptune Inc., 1964.

Jones, Robert C. *Two Feet to the Lakes*. Edmonds, WA: Pacific Fast Mail, 1993.

Lipman, Jean. *Rufus Porter Rediscovered*. New York: Clarkson N. Potter Inc./Publishers, 1980.

Mead, Edgar T. Jr. *Busted and Still Running*. Brattleboro, VT: Stephen Greene Press, 1968.

Monk, Guy M. *The Story of North Bridgton, Maine, 1761–1958*. Bridgton, ME: self-published, 1958.

Sargent, Porter. *A Handbook of Summer Camps*. Boston: self-published, 1925.

Visit us at
arcadiapublishing.com

Lightning Source UK Ltd.
Milton Keynes UK
UKHW052123261022
411161UK00004B/94